Black Sunday

Black Sunday: Dust Bowl Sonnets

Benjamin Myers

Literary Press
Lamar University

Copyright 2019 © Benjamin Myers
All Rights Reserved

ISBN: 978-1-942956-63-1
Library of Congress Control Number: 2018965367

Cover Photo: Arthur Rothstein
Author Photo: Zachary Riggin

Lamar University Literary Press
Beaumont, Texas

For my mother, Anna Myers, who taught me that a person can survive anything with faith, grit, and a good story.

Recent Poetry from Lamar University Literary Press

Bobby Aldridge, *An Affair of the Stilled Heart*
Michael Baldwin, *Lone Star Heart, Poems of a Life in Texas*
David Bowles, *Flower, Song, Dance: Aztec and Mayan Poetry*
Jerry Bradley, *Crownfeathers and Effigies*
Jerry Bradley and Ulf Kirchdorfer, editors, *The Great American Wise Ass Poetry Anthology*
Mark Busby, *Through Our Times: Occasional Poems 1960-2017*
Paul Christensen, *The Jack of Diamonds Is a Hard Card to Play*
Chip Dameron, *Waiting for an Etcher*
William Virgil Davis, *The Bones Poems*
Jeffrey DeLotto, *Voices Writ in Sand*
Chris Ellery, *Elder Tree*
Ken Hada, *Margaritas and Redfish*
Michelle Hartman, *Irony and Irrelevance*
Katherine Hoerth, *Goddess Wears Cowboy Boots*
Michael Jennings, *Crossings: A Record of Travel*
Gretchen Johnson, *A Trip Through Downer, Minnesota*
Ulf Kirchdorfer, *Chewing Green Leaves*
Janet McCann, *The Crone at the Casino*
Jim McGarrah, *The Truth About Mangoes*
Erin Murphy, *Ancilla*
Laurence Musgrove, *Local Bird*
Laurence Musgrove, *One Kind of Recording*
Godspower Oboido, *Wandering Feet on Pebbled Shores*
Carol Coffee Reposa, *Underground Musicians*
Jan Seale, *The Parkinson Poems*
Steven Schroeder, *the moon, not the finger, pointing*

For information on these and other Lamar University Literary Press books go to
www.Lamar.edu/literarypress

Acknowledgments

Poems in this volume first appeared, under different titles and often in earlier versions, in the following journals:

32 Poems, Dappled Things, Measure, Oklahoma Today, Rattle, San Pedro River Review, Windhover.

I am indebted to several good books on the topic of the dust bowl. Sanora Babb's novel *Whose Names are Unknown* is, in my opinion, superior even to Steinbeck's dust bowl classic in its humane depiction of the dust bowl farmers. Lawrence Svobida's *Farming the Dust Bowl* is an invaluable first-hand account by an intelligent, poetic, and admirably determined agriculturalist. Rilla Askew's *Harpsong* and Carter Revard's *Winning the Dust Bowl* both did much to stock my imagination. Of course, for many facts, I relied on Timothy Egan's fine book *The Worst Hard Time*. I also drew inspiration from Ken Burns' documentary, especially his interviews with those who experienced the dust themselves.

Images in this book are courtesy of Arthur Rothstein, photographer, Library of Congress, Public Domain.

CONTENTS

- 13 Part One: The Dust Bowl Sonnets
- 15 Dramatis Personae
- 17 Lily Burns Describes the Static in the Air
- 19 Will Burns Describes Plowing Early On and Later
- 20 The Reverend Describes the Sod Busters
- 21 Henry Describes the Duster
- 22 Interlude #1
- 23 Louise Burns Remembers the Suitcase Farmers
- 24 Ms. Manvel's Students Read Shelley's "Ozymandias"
- 25 The Reverend Thinks About His Work
- 27 Will Burns Discovers a Cow Down
- 28 Lily Burns Thinks About Her Wallpaper
- 29 Henry Reflects on the Dust Reaching Washington D.C.
- 30 Will Burns Reflects on Predators and Prey
- 31 Louise Burns Remembers the Rainmaker
- 32 Will Burns Describes the Grasshoppers
- 33 The Reverend on the Forced Wheat Burn
- 34 Ms. Manvel Visits a Missing Student with Dust Pneumonia
- 35 Lily Worries About Her Daughter
- 37 The Reverend Caught in a Duster Thinks of His Late Wife
- 38 The Reverend Describes His Eroding Congregation
- 39 Will Burns on the Great American Desert
- 41 Lily Describes the Crawlers
- 42 Lily Describes Real Loss
- 43 Will Tells How to Carry a Loss
- 44 Louis Burns Remembers the Gov't Cattle Slaughter
- 45 Will Describes Black Sunday
- 46 The Reverend Preaches a Sermon at Aaronson's Department Store
- 47 Ms. Manvel Describes the Dresses of Her Students

49 Will Lists His Assets on Another Loan Application
50 Interlude #2
51 The Reverend on Natural Theology
52 Will Tries to Describe Getting Caught in a Duster While Visiting His Mother's Grave
53 Lily Confronts the Gathering Crows
55 Henry Describes His Dreams
56 Will Thinks About Sunday Dinner
57 Lily Finds Odd Metaphors for Hope
58 Will's Aubade
59 The Reverend Describes the Rabbit Drive
60 Henry Misses the Exodusters
61 The Reverend Describes the Face of Christ in a Dust Cloud over Starvation Creek
62 Interlude #3
63 Lily Describes the Early Spring
65 Louise Burns Remembers the Foreclosure
66 Will Describes the Beginning of the Summer Wind
67 Will Thinks About Land Ownership
69 Henry Gets Used to the Dusters
71 Lily Describes the Penny Auction
73 The Reverend Talks to His Late Wife
74 The Reverend Complains to God
75 Ms. Manvel Tidies Up Her Classroom
76 Henry Describes Starvation Creek
77 The Reverend Hallucinates Flagellants
78 Henry Leaves with the Night Circus
79 Lily Describes Hope

83 Part Two: The Faith Healer

"By the sweat of your face you shall eat bread, till you return to the ground, for out of it you were taken; for you are dust, and to dust you shall return."
Genesis 3: 19

"No rifles are fired over new-made graves, no trumpets sound the 'Last Post,' for these are tragedies of peace, not war. These are not hero dead, they are merely the victims of the dust."
Lawrence Svobida, *Farming the Dust Bowl*

Part One: The Dust Bowl Sonnets

Dramatis Personae

Will Burns: A farmer in the Oklahoma Panhandle before, during, and after the Dust Bowl

Lily Burns: His wife

Louise Burns: Their Daughter, speaking later as an adult

Ms. Manvel: A teacher in a one-room schoolhouse

The Reverend: The local Presbyterian minister, a transplant from back east

Henry: The town drunk, who often sleeps in the Reverend's barn

"Autos have to turn on lights to penetrate gloom of dust storm. Amarillo, Texas."

Lily Burns Describes the Static in the Air

The static in the dust could knock a big
man down and stall a car mid-street, its dark
battery drained. Soon men learned how to rig
their cars with dragging chains to ground the spark.
Too late for us. We couldn't leave the town
at all, our truck not coming back from dead
without more money. Sitting there, the brown
Ford collected dust in its rusty bed.
That dust got higher every day and spilled
from the dead bed slowly, an hourglass
of sorts to keep count of what time we killed
by suffocation. Slowly day would pass.
At night I'd listen to the darkened plains
where cars, like angry ghosts, rattled their chains.

"A farmer listing his fields under the wind erosion control program. He receives twenty cents an acre for the work. Liberal, Kansas."

Will Burns Describes Plowing Early On and Later

As black as a cotton mouth's slick back, the soil
shined after plowing. As black as inside
a gunny sack, as black as motor oil.
I'd sit there on my tractor, full of pride.
That sweet, deep black turned green when shoots came out,
and, boy, I thought of money when I saw it.
I thought it'd turn to gold, if there's no drought.
Then we'd be in the black, is what I thought.
But every golden thing soon turned dead brown.
There weren't rain enough to fill a ditch.
That was when the gov't men came to town
and told us busted farmers all to hitch
our tractors up and drag our plows around,
furrowing dirt to catch the blowing ground.

The Reverend Describes the Sod Busters

After my Sally died I came out here
for peace but found the high plains like a river
in flood, the sod busters busting their sod
in breaking waves over the grassy plains.
Dang fool, I thought I could shake the Lord.
Riding the train, I watched the trees dwindle
and disappear, the sky grow broad like God's forehead
leaning toward that hard table-top of grass.
There is no place to hide. I took the job
I knew and preached to the busters of sod.
The soil was good, but they busted up too much.
The wind picked up. The ground began to blow:
the earth scraped bare of skin, like some flayed saint,
a land, like me, torn open to its God.

Henry Describes the Duster

The Reverend says that I was in my cups.
Hell, I was in the barn. Drinking. It came
up like a murder ghost, that dust, the same
as it had come before, but now it ups
and doubles, wind whining like coyote pups
about to howl. And me, all jake-leg lame,
top-heavy, wobbling to shut the dad-blamed
barn door. I don't get there. The dust erupts
like Daddy would with strength enough to knock
a grown bull down and grit to scour its hide.
That dust will blind a man in seconds, won't it?
I fell and hit my head on some damn rock.
The Reverend says we've all got shine inside.
You crack your head and light comes out, why don't it?

Interlude #1

Driving through
the panhandle
today, you see the great wind
turbines turning
slowly
like white birds
stepping over the small
bones of ghost towns.

Louise Burns Remembers the Suitcase Farmers

These fancy sons-a-bitches come down here
from somewhere back east, suitcase in their hands,
just stepping off the train and planting wheat,
then gone as ghosts until the harvest time.
My daddy seen one yank with polished shoes
and a silk tie straddling his tractor, soft
hand holding down his little city hat.
"I didn't know to laugh or shoot," he said.
He must have laughed, I guess, cause no one's dead
that weren't already dead. Well, I recall
those fields so full of hairy wheat. It looked
to me like cricket legs, a Bible swarm
of them. But later it was all just dirt,
and only us left here to breathe it.

Ms. Manvel's Students Read Shelley's "Ozymandias"

The poem conjures up their own dry land,
I guess. Those "vast and trunkless legs of stone"
could be their fathers' silos stuck in sand.
Behind their little desks they grow a frown.
I smile at them, regret my rash command
they memorize the poem we just read.
They know enough of dust and time, these things
already blown clean through their under-fed
young bones. I smooth my dress. It would appear
that I've misstepped. The vanity of kings
does not mean much to children who despair
of ever eating beef again. Decay,
after all, has left their homes paintless, stripped bare
by heaving hills of sand rolling and rolling away.

The Reverend Thinks About His Work

I haven't raised a blessed thing. Not beans, not corn,
and not the dead. I've seen a ranch hand reach
into the square end of a cow, the new-born
calf pulled out wet as laundry. I preach
but no new life unchannels from the old.
Still-born, my words like heavy buck-shot fall
out of the barrel, rust to red on the cold
bare wood church floor. I want to save them all.
I can't. My church is not the ark. The dust
is not a flood. It's God's turned back, not wrath.
Neglect, distraction, not divine sword thrust:
His grace grown up in weeds that hide the path.
I drop my words into the slots of dry,
cold wind, then lose them in the tin-gray sky

and let the sleeping dead lie.

"Stock watering hole almost completely covered by shifting topsoil. Cimarron County, Oklahoma."

Will Burns Discovers a Cow Down

At first I thought she was a clump of thistle
blowed up against the fence, but then I seen
the eye, half closed, dark, staring from the gristle
and knew we had a Hereford down. A mean
storm had been blowing just before, but now
the sky was clear. Stooping down in the dried
earth there, I scared the crows from off the cow
and ran my hand along her boney side.
I couldn't find a bite or bullet hole
explaining how it was that she went down.
Her hide was worn but seemed unbroken, whole
but weathered like dead grass to patchy brown.
Then when I slit the belly's scoured hide,
sand spilled out from the desert dammed inside.

Lily Burns Thinks About her Wallpaper

The flowers on the wallpaper have gone,
buried by gritty layers of black dust
pushed through the gaps around the door and blown
onto the walls and furniture like rust.
I picked that paper out myself and hung
the flowered strips I'd brushed with heavy paste
so we'd have springtime always here among
the empty places of this grassy waste.
But now the flowers like Will's crops have sunk
beneath the thirsty dirt that makes it all
the same, and, like I'm locked up in a trunk,
the dust dark makes it hard to see the wall
no matter how I try, how hard I stare.
But still I know what I don't see is there.

Henry Reflects on the Dust Reaching Washington D.C.

Today I heard the dust done reached the dome
back east, the one them senators sit under
debating how to stop our home sweet home
from blowing up their nose. It makes me wonder
how much of here will have to end up there—
how high the dust will climb them marble steps—
before the suited ones decide they care.
Don't know about them senators and reps
but this here post where I been leaning knows
we're halfway there and past already now
when every puffed up gust of wind that blows
turns up more earth than any tractor plow.
But by the time our dirt has smudged their shiny shoes
we'll all be buried here and last week's news.

Will Burns Reflects on Predators and Prey

I think about the killing things
out here that we don't see. The rattlers, sure,
and copperheads and scorpions: the pure
mean hunter hidden till it bites or stings.
But all them things is dying too. Wind brings
down dust to crush their heads. No prey to lure
them out, they starve in holes, or else they cure
on sun hot rocks. I guess their dying means
that everything has something that can chew
it up. That there's the fact we've got to stand
to stay out here and keep on our two feet.
We close our door at night with nothing left to do
but listen to the moaning of the land
when windy night opens its mouth to eat.

Louise Burns Remembers the Rainmaker

They brung this Yankee man down here to make
it rain with rockets fired into the clouds
and dynamite tied to balloons. He'd take
a stick of TNT, wave back the crowds
of farmers' wives, us scrawny kids, then light
the fuse and just let go. His fire would rise
on wicks beneath balloons, dim in that bright
hot mid-day sun. The sparks were thick as flies
falling on kids and farmers' wives. Then boom
and nothing more. No rain. No, not so much
as one small, spitty drop. The crop of broom
corn kept on withering; the wheat stayed dry to touch.
Flat cloud on flat sky like a sheet and stain.
There ain't no man can make it rain.

Will Burns Describes the Grasshoppers

They ate through shovel handles, left the blades
behind like chicken bones and made the fence posts shine
with crawling when the wheat was gone. I laid
out traps with kerosene, saw dust, strychnine,
but they still swarmed, a shifting cloud overhead
like sand beneath our feet. With nothing more
to eat—the oats, the corn, the wheat all dead—
they'd chew the shirt right off your back, eat your
boots from your feet, the pants from off your leg.
They crawled at first, but then down here they flew.
The preacher says they're like the Pharaohs' plague.
I told him then that I must be a Jew:
We liked to call this land a sea of wheat—
Look, now it parts in hops before my feet.

The Reverend on the Forced Wheat Burn

The binder dropped the bundles and they rolled
like men whose arms are tied behind their backs.
Like saints, the excess sheaves were set ablaze.
Like martyrs the extra sheaves of wheat were burned.
Some tried to cheat, but his mistake was honest—
he grew a few more acres than he meant
and would not get his check unless he could
reduce his yield to what the county set.
He offered up his wheat to feed the skin—
on bone-faced folk who walked the hungry road.
The county agent said the wheat must burn.
They lit the stacks; there rose a smoky dust,
the fire rustling like shuffled paperwork,
the kernels crackling like a crazed applause.

Ms. Manvel Visits a Missing Student with Dust Pneumonia

They hung wet blankets on the door and all
the window panes to stop the blowing dust.
The child coughed from her small bed against the wall.
Her mama soaked a rag to clean the crust
of spit, blood, dirt, and sweat that grew on her
sharp chin. Her daddy stood beside the cot
and listened to the grainy wind, its roar
of dirt against the quilts. As asked, I brought
them kerosene to mix with turpentine
and lard to spread across her chest. She hacked
and coughed so hard it shook her bones like pine
trees in high wind, like wind around that shack.
Her daddy said, *A break come in this dust,*
we'll bury her down where the dried creek was.

Lily Worries About Her Daughter

The windmill spins its shadow on bare yard
where Louise sits drawing pictures in dirt.
I watch through the dusty kitchen window.
The thing I worry most about is her.
She has a hardness in her ways. She draws
these little houses, little barns and fields
then scoops up little fistfuls of dirt and drops
it on the Oklahoma she just made.
The thing I fret the most about is her.
I run the dampened cloth across her face
at night, wring it over the porcelain bowl.
The water's brown before I've washed her ears.
She doesn't seem to know she wears the dust
or that she's the thing that worries me the most.

"Dust storm. Oklahoma"

The Reverend Caught in a Duster Thinks of His Late Wife

A hill of dust I am not in so much
as under, shovelfuls of dirt dropped hard
on my body. I lay in the church-yard
and could not see, six feet away, the church.
I thought that I was in my grave and cried
because they buried me so far from her,
to have so much dumb earth between me here
and the one I meant to always sleep beside.
But after long moments of dark, the storm
moved on, a demented grave-yard digger bent
on filling all the world with interment,
a globe of graves fresh-dug, mounded, still warm.
Weighted with dirt, it took what strength I've got
to stand again. I rose and she did not.

The Reverend Describes His Eroding Congregation

Like fields my congregation bit by bit
eroded. Stripped by wind. Gust-flayed and gone.
The hymns began to dry up like the creeks,
the old pump-organ dead as cattle bones.
Come Sunday, I'd open the church at six
and sit in a back pew to wait. By ten,
the dust permitting, folks, a few, would come
to sit a spell and hear the word, such as
I had. But fewer came each time I preached.
Most could not make it in. I dreamt the wind
picked them up one by one and bore them east
or west or just away, a cloud of gray.
The Bible says that man is but the dust.
The wind will have its way with all of us.

Will Burns on the Great American Desert

A desert waste is what this place is now
and all it's ever going to be. The land
ain't ours. Blowing over itself, the sand
will take it back. The rain follows the plow
men said, but then it didn't rain. The cow,
the buffalo, Indian, and ranch hand
should have it back, and can, if they can stand
to live here now the dirt's begun to blow.
But I ain't got no place to go. I'll stay
and let that mean old sun burn me new shades of brown.
I'll let the blowing sand eat at my skin
until my outside layer's blown away
and nothing's left but muscle and raw bone.
I was a man, once. What will I be then?

"Abandoned farm in the dust bowl area. Oklahoma"

Lily Describes the Crawlers

The scratching of the centipedes' hard legs
and scritch of wasps and beetles as they bore
into the sod house boards forced us to pour
boiling water down the walls to kill their eggs.
So, then we built a real farm house. With beds
above the ground, I thought we'd sleep. But more
and more dirt blew. I taped the windows and the door
to stop dust, bugs, and starving copperheads.
Now lying in my iron bed at night,
I see behind my eyes the child's pout,
jack rabbit wild and daddy longlegs thin,
as touchy as a hard scratched chigger bite.
I spend my days keeping the crawlers out,
but worry more on what I can't keep in.

Lily Describes Real Loss

The ruined blanket, midnight blood, the squeeze
like iron hands around my middle parts,
the quiet afterwards. Will on his knees
to scrub the wet floor boards. Things worse than dust.
This was my first time through, before Louise.
That's why I still don't call the girl my first
or only. Farmer's wives are made for grief,
I think, like seeds and clouds are made to burst.
Out by the barn, a huddled bunch of pine,
the ponderosas growing only here.
Beneath the trees the boy I call mine
still is buried. The rest of us are near.
We keep a grief like dust the rough winds bring:
it settles in the cracks in everything.

Will Tells How to Carry a Loss

Every farmer knows you carry what you lose
one season to the next. If hoppers eat your wheat,
the corn stalks scorch to brittle bones, you use
accounting tricks to make it come out neat.
You carry loss in green-lined books, you haul
it in your hollowed stomach pit. You sit
on the edge of your iron bed in iron dawn and pull
your ragged boots on, pick up your loss and get
to work. You carry loss like it's a bucket full
of water you can't spill, a lead pipe slung across your back.
In bed, you rest it on your chest—the dull
weight flattens out your breath and makes your lungs go slack.
In twos, like heavy logs, you haul it with your wife,
and carry it for all your God-given life.

Louise Burns Remembers the Gov't Cattle Slaughter

They dug a ditch out past the north-side fence
then clapped, shouted, slapped the brittle, bone-stretched hide
and made the big, dumb things to run against
their will into the ditch where they all died.
My daddy flinched with every shot, but I
stood still and small and waited there beside
the trough. I prayed to God he wouldn't cry
and cracked the grass beneath my feet where it had dried.
Since then I've buried two good men, stood twice
before the Baptist preacher as a bride;
I've hit and washed three sons and picked their lice,
lost money, men, and hope, the rags of pride,
but can't erase the way they twitched and bled

Will Describes Black Sunday

We'd done shot most the herd by then,
so all I had to do was feed
that thin and boney barnyard hen
we kept for eggs and fed on seed.
But it weren't scratching 'round the yard.
It'd gone to roost like it was night.
The dust hit me sudden and hard
like a man who's looking to fight.
By then I couldn't find my way
back to the door I'd just walked through,
so I dropped down and there I lay
while dirt poured on and hot wind blew.
When I got up my eyes was hurt.
And all I saw was dirt.

The Reverend Preaches a Sermon at Aaronson's Department Store

Bristled with guns they marched to Hershel's, the German
Jew who kept decent folks in decent clothes
by losing his own shirt. They aimed to close
his store, break windows, called him "Jewish vermin."
I don't know how it is that they determined
to blame the only Jew anyone here knows.
I worked my way between shovels and hoes,
stood on the counter, gave—at last—a sermon:
Let's make of our stone hearts a wailing wall
and plant our knees for prayer in this here dirt.
No ashes for mourning, so wear the dust.
Before it rains again, you know, we'll all
know what it is to wander in the desert
or else to have it wander over us.

Ms. Manvel Describes the Dresses of Her Students

The girls wear dresses sown from old feed sacks,
dotted with little blue flowers, blowsy.
Their mamas keep good clothes on their poor backs
and make a little up from their lousy
luck. Gingham, floral, checked, and plain: they've sewed
whatever pattern of the sacks they've had.
No matter how one's failed or what one's owed,
a pretty dress can make a girl less sad,
I think. The more the dust comes down, the more
they sew, use every sack that they can find.
Long dark days, daughters sit on broomed dirt floor,
watch needles moving through deft hands and mind.
And when one died, they gathered sacks and chose
to dress her in the one with white primrose.

"These farm implements should never have been used for they destroyed a naturally rich grazing area. Mills, New Mexico"

Will Lists His Assets on Another Loan Application

800 acres of itch, grit, and chirr
crawling with hoppers, burning like a match.
All mine. The foot deep drifts of dirt that were
my neighbor's field, mine too now, since I catch
with my strip lists the dirt he don't do much
to keep. The tractor with the rear wheels stuck
halfway in sand I owe your bank a bunch
on still and won't pay off unless my luck
turns. But it won't. We shot the little herd.
The truck is dead. Your bank has got the car.
The combine's broke. I guess I've got my word,
and next to that my other assets are
dirt sore eyes, overalls with one knee hole,
a body dressed in rags, a ragged soul.

Interlude #2

The fields had breathed with wheat
the way a man breathes
in his sleep, deep rising
falling peace.

Now neither the land nor any man
it dreams can catch
a breath, despite the frantic wind.

The Reverend on Natural Theology

Seeing God in nature do
you see Him crucified? The rabbit ripped
by dogs, its guts strewn across a crew-
cut field, the hide left wet where it was stripped?
Driving through countryside you sometimes see
a line of coyote pelts hung from barbed fence,
flapped by high wind, bothered with flies and flea
infested, bullet holes in all the skins.
Do you then read the Book of Nature's red
ink dribbled down the posts? Consider all
the world's wide gore, the white-tailed deer that's spread
across the road, the earth's unlapped offal.
Everything broken must be broken again.
I will make you fissures of men.

Will Tries to Describe Getting Caught in a Duster While Visiting His Mother's Grave

   dead got deeper   forget
where they   . The tops of tombstones
from sand   grit
like snapper backs in mud   .
               little saw blades
sudden   duster   caught
   felt my way down fence
stumbled   thistles   hot.
Where they was buried back there
        a house someone   empty
   felt   floor   one thing
      old pair of shoes   any
      blind again   dies.
And when I made it home, my woman washed my eyes.

Lily Confronts the Gathering Crows

I don't believe a thing the crows are saying
when they kazoo the squinty sun at evening.
All that crowish twitching, raspy braying,
and side-step fidget doesn't mean a thing.
Not death. They sure ain't squawking death. What if
that crazy hag across the creek says so?
She's just mad that her boy was born all stiff
down one side, that he has to walk so slow
while our girl runs like water over rocks,
like clouds on storm wind, rays of sun on wheat.
I'm sad for her, but we all have to take our knocks.
Sometimes, while my girl sleeps, I bless her feet.
The crows aren't words. I sure won't read their feathers.
I'll keep my child, and God can keep his own dark letters.

"Liberal (vicinity), Kan. Soil blown by dust bowl winds piled up in large drifts on a farm"

Henry Describes His Dreams

I blab a fear of glowing old. Who sleeps
like that, all lit inside and out afire?
I like the way the last light leaks and creeps
across the dust-bit barn floor. Gone too far
the folks I knew. They needed wings. They got
out. Dream, I say I did, about the bones
that up and walked. The cattle that they shot,
it walked again without its skin. The moans
and moos hung on the moon like hairy moss,
dropped down onto the dirt and there it bloomed
a grass so green it split the night. The loss
comes at you in your dreams and there it looms.
Ah, well, it's what's there and not that bites
no matter where you sleep these dusty nights.

Will Thinks About Sunday Dinner

A can of beans is about the only thing
the dust ain't in before you open it.
You eat them fast, then wipe the dusty ring
of grease around your mouth. The dust has hit
us hard as far as Sunday dinner goes.
My Lily tries to set the table pretty,
her grandma's china, blue and white. Dirt blows
all over it and leaves the settings gritty.
Most food we swallow kindly whole before
the dust can get too much in it, but still
we swallow lots of dirt and swallow more
in muddy cups pumped from what was our well.
But if this dust is ever done, I'll sit
and eat a whole fried chicken, chewing every bit.

Lily Finds Odd Metaphors for Hope

I can't remember feeling clean:
a freshly washed white pillowcase,
a meadow green with summer rain,
a freshly swept and dusted house.
I feel like dried and shed snake skin,
left in the dirt next to the rock
the rattler wriggled up against
to scrape the scales from its long back.
But, if I'm just the skin it shed,
what is the snake that with its fresh
new case crawls up the dry creek bed
to cool in shade its new scraped flesh?
If I'm the husk, a raspy rope,
the fresh and new born snake's my hope.

Will's Aubade

Across the plains this dark, this kindly cave-mouth
morning, the men and wives are breaking up
the ice so animals can drink, dropping
wood mauls and axes in the frozen trough.
This is what's given here. This be the cup.

I know. I've strung my life out on these plains;
I've walked my length of years like line of fence
with nothing on my left or right but stains
of scattered cloud in shadow on the grass,
bumps of gopher dirt dead weeds have blown against.

The sunrise fog that foots the stacked hay bales
and pools around the scrubby line of trees
makes pasture look like sea-front property,
the scattered bales like surface-breaking whales,
but we're eight-hundred miles from the sea.

The Reverend Describes the Rabbit Drive

The dust-black blocks of town swayed, moved, and breathed
heaving breaths of jack rabbit like a hurt
animal's panting side. The bare fields seethed
with hungry rabbits driven from the dirt:
a hundred-thousand jacks swarming through town
like twitching, scrawny end-time horses loosed
by all our sins. They swallowed up the brown
plants scorched by static in the air and bruised
the dust with thudding jumps. The men gave me,
the women, and the boys something to hit
with—busted axe handles, fence posts, a tree
limb—and they said that we were not to quit
until dead jacks in piles filled the street
with fevered meat, diseased, unsafe to eat.

Henry Misses the Exodusters

The empty houses. Skulls, you know. They look.
I sleep or fall in any skull I want.
I liked the one the passing freight train shook
one night all through. But then I guess it burnt.
I wasn't smoking. Much. Most times the wells
are dry. I look down those earth throats and think
I'd like to fall deep dark into some fresh hells.
But don't mind me. I think I need a drink.
The houses though. They start to lean a bit
when no one lives in them. I guess we all
do that. The folks may leave; a house won't quit
until the dirty wind downs its last wall.
I sleep there in the bones of people's homes.
I sleep here in the bones.

The Reverend Describes the Face of Christ in a Dust Cloud over Starvation Creek

When we first saw the face of Jesus in
the dust, we knew he'd come to judge us all,
riding a cloud of choking blackened wind
over the brittle grass and cattle skulls.
He hung above the town from dawn past noon,
absorbed the bitter heat, then blurred
at dusk. Dissolved beside the hidden sun,
our Lord seemed neither risen nor interred.
And then the sudden frenzy of the word,
the praying, screeching mess. The preachers did
the best they could to conjure up the blood
beneath that beard, the wrath, the gore-soaked wood.
By then seemed none who saw that bearded face
supposed that it could be a sign of grace.

Interlude #3

The coyote's
yellow eyes,
like two bare
bulbs
hanging
in two dim empty rooms.

When he yawns
his throat
is the longest, darkest hallway
you have ever walked down.

Lily Describes the Early Spring

You almost think the dust
is gone, the world of rust-
brown red dissolved in light,
when morning sun's this bright
and weightless, like a cake
un-iced or mountain lake
clear, deep, and fresh. I sweep
our floor. The dust motes leap
inside of sun that falls
through windows onto walls.
You'd catch a glimpse and whiff
of growing grasses if
you step outside and blink.
That's what you almost think.

"Furrowing against the wind to check the drift of sand. Dust Bowl, north of Dalhart, Texas"

Louise Burns Remembers the Foreclosure

A cottonmouth you knew by how it stank
and rattlers by their sound. But ain't no way
of warning for the snake they call "the bank"
until you reach down in its hole and pay.
The sheriff, bald as a trailer hitch,
took off his hat like somebody had died.
My daddy called him a son-of-a-bitch,
while mama stood behind the door and cried.
Then I went out to watch the tumbleweed
crowd up like cows against the back fence line.
I sat against the shed to throw sand stones
at rotten posts and watch the sunset bleed,
and knew the things your heart looks at and moans
"that's mine"
is different from the things a person owns.

Will Describes the Beginning of the Summer Wind

The windmill like a turkey with its fanned
tail feathers roosted on its perch above
the barn, not moving much until it turned
hard suddenly, a hot wind starting up
from somewhere down the burning throat of drouth.
What wheat we had then soon began to cook
right on the stalk. The squawk of dragging metal
ripped the quiet summer day to shreds,
the oil on the turbine gritted up
with dust. That wind breathed down our necks for weeks
then stopped one day like a man whose heart gives out
while working. Nothing moved. The whole panhandle
was like a ship stuck on a stagnant sea
or like a car half-buried in a ditch.

Will Thinks About Land Ownership

If any ghosts are in this dirt, it's them
we took it from that haunts it. Only fair.
I thought I saw their horses in the cloud
of dust that dropped on us. I thought I heard
a war cry in the ripping wind. The land's
not ours. We're like the tumbleweed that hid
in seed that shipped from overseas and now
runs thick as bandit gangs across the plains.
Or maybe we're like hoppers in a plague
who eat the world to brown bones and move on.
Before the duster dropped, the tire tracks
along the road and out were clear and deep.
The dirt storm gone, I'd swear I saw the marks
of warriors' horses half-mooned in the dust.

"Dust storm. It was conditions of this sort which forced many farmers to abandon the area. Spring 1935. New Mexico"

Henry Gets Used to the Dusters

The aerial line glows red with static
charge from the dust and looks like a scar
down God's own thigh of darkened sky. Frantic
birds try to fly ahead but don't get far.
There's lightning in the dirt, the crooked teeth
of a dark mouth. Mean jawed. And to the south
the field begins to boil: rabbits beneath
drouth starved scrub run from that hungry mouth.
I've stepped onto the sandy tongue to feel
it undulate in speech. But what it said
I can't tell you. Or I forgot. The real
point is it talks. The aerial line glows red
from windmill tower to house. It snaps and moans.
The birds that fall? God's broken finger bones.

"Discouraged farmers have been leaving this area over a period of years, leaving their heavy equipment in the fields. Mills, New Mexico"

Lily Describes the Penny Auction

The pale, the weathered gathered like a murder
of crows, by one and two, out by the barn:
the men with guns and shovels, our neighbors,
some folks from church, a few of our thin kin.
The auctioneer stood on the wagon bed,
rambled his voice across the names of all
our things: hay rack, plow, tractor, binder. Dead
silence was all the bid to meet his call,
except when Will yelled out "a penny," "dime,"
or "nickel." By the end, the auctioneer
himself was laughing, closing the bids each time
Will called. The land is ours now, free and clear,
a gift from men who would have shot, I'm guessing,
had someone bid and hindered their rough blessing.

"West Texas 'family farm.' On edge of the Dust Bowl"

The Reverend Talks to His Late Wife

Almost all we grasp of Heaven is
like baseball on the radio,
a field somewhere of actual grass
and actual dirt we only know
through talk. The players on the field
are there, but we don't see them play.
Their actions, whether lame or skilled,
exist to us in what announcers say.
And yet sometimes I dream not just
your face but your whole being close
and feel as if I've walked through dust
choked fields into a poplar copse
with suddenly a presence there
of wild thing like elk or deer.

The Reverend Complains to God

Dry farmers, God,
in this dry age
have stripped the sod.
No pilgrimage,
no holy sign
revives the creek,
no word divine
breaks up the streak
of dust dead wells,
of dirty gloom
and sandy swells.
No martyrdom
here, just the boot
that tears up grass
by scrawny root.

Ms. Manvel Tidies Up Her Classroom

I dust the little classroom things, the chairs—
frail rickety bone-like things—shelves of paints,
books, toys, and puzzles: brush the dusty layers
from primers and their grammar, cleaning up their *aints*,
their *thems*, their *wuzzes*. How I make them shine!
These kids are mine. I notice when they miss
and check on them because I'll keep what's mine
protected from the dust. I promise this
now. Afternoons the light comes slanting red
through western windows, holds the floating dust
suspended. "Terrible beauty," Yeats said.
The children gape at it, until I bust
their reverie to give a spelling test.
The war with dust oblivion won't give us any rest.

Henry Describes Starvation Creek

This creek running tip-toe through sage and tall
grass gets a little broader further down
and shoulders through the thread-bare little town
that bears its name. But I don't cross at all
in town, since Daddy always said a ghost
can't cross fast moving water. I got spooks
to leave behind each time I cross, dead folks
and lost ones. Witness clouds. A spectral host
that don't shut up. My barn's all full of birds.
So, when I crossed, I crossed up here. The bed,
though, now's gone dry. Through their teeth the dead will speak
on now no matter where I cross. Stone words.
The tops of the drowning heads of all my dead,
the rocks in the bed of dried Starvation Creek.

The Reverend Hallucinates Flagellants

A line of men stripped to the waist walked out
of dirt black dark at what would be the dusk
if dust had not swallowed the day, beating
themselves with strips of rawhide tied with bits
of bone. (I wonder now if it was real).
They groaned and chanted something low and blurred,
trudged their thin line like a dead snake dragged through
the dirt. It hurt to watch them flick the whip
back over their own backs as if to lick
the blood with tongues of leather. While I stood
on the church porch and watched them pass, the street
was empty otherwise: just this procession
trying to tear whatever sin brought us
the dust from under their own bone-stretched skin.

Henry Leaves with the Night Circus

Clown peeping through a crack into my barn:
white face. Stiff breeze flaps circus tent outside.
All day I'm liquid. Stand up. I can't. Damn
my bones, all wet. Ain't time to get them dried.
I reckon that it's heat that makes them start
the circus up at night. The clouds all beard
the moon, like lady. Organ notes that dart
into my barn like mice. Elephants afeard.
Stand up. I can, now. Go and see the acts.
Old lion tamer with his whip and chair,
those sequined girls standing on horses' backs,
a tight-rope lady toeing through dark air.
They've pulled now tent stakes out, loaded the crew
to leave by night. I think I'm going too.

Lily Describes Hope

A summer day was like a heavy feather
those first few years, weighty and soft. The light
got into everything and then shone out.
The fields was like a lamp in sleepy weather.
But drowsy heat soon turned to something tougher,
mean like a man who's drunk and wants to fight.
We lost the rain. We sweated through the night.
You grab on crazy hope, if you're a mother.
Then, one day, drops make circles in the dirt.
You run outdoors to feel the rain again.
After so many scratchy years of drouth,
you open up your mouth to taste the wet.
Just sprinkles but, funny, a little rain
and you can almost see it, the new earth.

Part Two: The Faith Healer

The Faith Healer

Her hands were I.V. bruised and spotted blue
with brown. Her cotton gown was almost paper.
In bare linoleum-inflected light,
she listed left, one elbow on the metal
armrest of her wheelchair, sitting there propped
lopsided like a bag of onions.

The nurse had wheeled her out to talk to me,
a volunteer ear, someone to sit nearby
and hear what stories she had saved, had stacked
in canning jars on shelves that were her mind.

It was the final year of the Great War.
We girls was only ten or so that summer,
me and my best friend, Lily. Lord, the heat!
Hot as blazes. I'd go out to chores each morning
and come back wrung with sweat by lunch. My clothes
was ruined with it. Dust too! It got so bad
I coughed it up. It got so that a body
could barely breath. It didn't rain at all.
The little swimming hole we had us turned
belly up into a muddy puddle by the middle
of July. And then it just went dry. My Daddy,
when he come in from working every night,

would say that God is surely punishing us.
Maybe He was. But I don't know just what
we done.

        We couldn't swim. It got too hot
to do much else, and so we got a little club
started up, just for us girls, had a treehouse
off up in the scrubby woods behind my place.
We made the clubhouse from whatever junk
was left around: an old barn door we jammed
between two branches of the trunk, old tires
for stools, a knotted rope we pulled up after us.
You had to know the password to get
it lowered back. The password—Lord—was Whiskey!

Lily and me was up in that tree-
house one hot Sunday after church, just combing
and brushing out our dolls' hair when that black
Nettie Collins comes slowly circling round
the trunk of that old tree. We didn't pay
her any mind until she started up
whispering, *whiskey, whiskey, whisky,*
a hoarse and throaty kind of whisper-shout.

Well, Lily and me just stared at each other,
our eyes all round and big. Where did she get
the password? Lily put her doll down then,
carefully smoothing its calico dress
beneath it when she laid it on the boards,

and said, I do believe that girl will go
on whispering whiskey until we let
her up. I shrugged and lowered down the rope.
We couldn't have no one overhearing
our password. Don't know where that black girl got
it from. We looked down from our floor of boards
and watched her slowly climb the knotted rope.

And then it broke.

                        The fall wasn't that far
but wasn't nothing. Nettie laid there, still
and quiet. Like a fallen branch landed
in leaves and uncut grass. I got real scared.

I didn't want her hurt or nothing. But
I didn't want to be in trouble neither.
I didn't want no one to think we done
it to that girl on purpose, which we most certainly
did not, since we was just little girls ourselves
and weren't no experts on tying knots.

We shimmied down that tree as fast as we
could go. That rough old bark scraped up my legs
read bad. Lily wasn't saying nothing.
She ran right up to Nettie and dropped down
next to her, put her hands on Nettie's hands
and started praying hard beneath her breath.

Now I don't know still to this day just what
she said. It was a soft and mumbling sound,
an engine chugging far away somewhere.
But she was praying hard, something repeated
again and again beneath her breath.
Then Nettie opened up her eyes and said
"whiskey." Some folks said later Nettie was
not hurt so bad, but I knew her for dead.
Yes, I knew her for dead. That was the first.

We didn't play at that tree-house no more
and wouldn't have the time to if we wanted.
That's cause I couldn't keep my big mouth shut
and blabbed all over town how Lily saved
that girl. Most folks ignored us anyway.
They said that it was girlish foolishness.
But old man Morris had a little boy
real sick with something doctors couldn't name
and came out to her Daddy's place to find
Lily and ask her to pray for that boy.
And I was there when he came walking up,
his sad old face unshaved, his eyes sunk in
like dried up wells. He held the boy in his thin arms
like taters in a sack and looked with begging eyes
at Lily. We weren't nothing but small girls.
We'd been down to the pasture blowing heads
off dandelions, jumping over cow
patties, and now we was there in her mamma's yard
throwing pebbles at chickens just to watch

them bob and peck. I reckon no one would
have said nothing if we just turned and climbed
back over the fence into the pasture grass.

But Lily didn't turn away. Instead
she walked right up to where he held the boy
and put her little hand across his head
and started praying hard and quiet again.
Old Morris stood there waiting for the Ghost
to come and heal his little boy. The sweat
ran down his leathery face and made circles
in the dust around his feet. And Lily kept
on praying. Maybe Morris heard the words
she used, and maybe Jesus heard them too,
but all I heard was mumbling, like a bee
caught in a jar. I saw her move her lips
and squeeze her eyes tight shut. The boy rasped out
a little cough. And that was it. A squirrel
rustled tree limbs up overhead, and Morris
nodded once, turned, and walked back up that dusty road.
 Then Lily sighed and went inside the house.

Not three days later I saw that boy out playing
baseball and running barefoot through the dirt.
His daddy went all over town to tell
what Lily did. I never knowed just what
that boy had, but mamma said he was real sick,
and everyone said that Lily made him well.
Seemed then like everybody needed something healed.

Not just children but the old folks too
was brought around for Lily's prayers. Some men
brought in sick wives. Some women brought their men.
A farmer brought a bloated-up old cow
and asked if Lily'd pray for it to live.

Her mamma and her daddy were dumbstruck
and felt they should protect their little girl
from all that throbbing hurt and desperate need.
But then they couldn't keep their Lily hid.
They put her in the barn, but some old woman
whose husband had raging pneumonia sniffed
her out and made her pray. They hid her at the church,
a little room in back, until the ladies'
Tuesday morning bible study saw her mamma
sneaking in a bowl of beans for Lily's supper.
So soon it seemed there was no way to keep
the healer from the people needing healing.

Now, Lily's daddy was a hard man, no
church going man. Lily's mamma would get on
to him for staying home on Sunday, beg
him just to go with her to church one time,
but he would just get stony in the eyes
and say, "God can come here if he wants me,"
and she would say, "Well he just might."
Well, like I said, he was a stony man
but loved his daughter like nothing I'd seen,
which made me kindly wish he was my daddy,

no matter everybody said he's mean
as Hell. Excuse me. What he did was tear
an old hen house down, start to build a stage
right in the patchy yard beside their house
He walled the stage up on three sides and stretched
chicken wire across the front so no
one could get in unless he let them through
a door he cut into one wall. He put
a little chair in there so Lily could
sit down. It took him two whole days under
that hot, mean sun before the stage was done.

Well, we was sitting in the church Sunday,
fanning ourselves and sweating up our best clothes.
The preacher with his coat took off, his sleeves
rolled up, was working up to his big finish
about how some don't think that Hell is real
until they feel the flames around their feet.
And I could see Ms. Molly Smith, the spinster
piano player, start to stretch her fingers
to play the alter call, when everybody turned
to see who just came bursting through the doors
behind the pews. And there stood Lily's daddy
dripping with sweat. Ms. Molly dropped her hands
from over the piano keys. His face
as set as brick, he said, "Well, if you folks
want healing come and get it over with."

The preacher never gave that alter call,
cause everybody jumped up and ran home
to get their sick, or else just went along
to see. Then word got out and other churches
stopped in the middle of their meetings too
and came to see the healing and be healed.
I never saw so many folks, besides
the county fair, before, and, like a fair,
there was an air of danger and excitement.
Some children got a game of tag going,
and ran between the grownups there to see
the miracles that they had heard about.
And ladies from the Methodist Church brought pies
and started selling them for a fund-raiser,
which wasn't right, because she was our healer.

He'd never made a plan for who'd get healed
first, second, third and on, and people started
to push a little. Lily sat there on
her chair and folks was crowding against the wire
her daddy nailed across the stage. He stood
tall with his shotgun slung across his arm,
staring the crowd down, trying hard to think
of what to do. But then the preacher stepped
up to the door, and Lily's daddy let
him in. And just like that the preacher took
the whole thing over. Just mad that his best
Hell sermon got cut short, is what I think,
and wanting, then, to be important-like.

The preacher stood on the stage and tilted back
his head at Heaven and began to pray.
"Just show me who you want to heal, oh Lord,"
he said with eyes squeezed shut, the sun shining
on his bald head. And then he raised his arm
and swung it like a weather vane. He stopped
and opened up his eyes to see who he
had pointed out. "God says it's you," he said
still pointing where he'd stopped, and so the first
one healed was Rachel Jones who had a rash
all down one side of her whole face. A deacon
helped her up to the stage, where Lily's daddy
still managed who got in. And things went on
like that from there. Each time someone came up
the crowd would grow real quiet, but I don't know
why because no one heard a thing. Lily would get
to moving her pale lips and squeezing shut
her eyes. To me it looked like she was hurting too.
And even though the preacher said that we
should close our eyes and bow our heads, the most
of us just watched. Once, waiting for the next
one chosen to come up, I caught Lily's eye,
and she looked like she could just cry, but didn't.
She kept on praying through that day and then
again the next and kept it up all week.

It wasn't like it is on television,
with men in fancy suits and people falling
down when the healer touches them. Lily

wasn't tapping no one on the head
or shouting things about the Holy Ghost.
The sick ones just came up, or else was carried
up there, and Lily prayed, and then they left,
either healed or not, I guess. And I can't say
if everyone she prayed for then got healed.
I can't because I didn't know them all.
Folks came from all around just for the chance
of being healed. So I can't say they was
or wasn't when they went away. But some
I know from hereabouts was healed. Like Joe,
the grocer's boy who had the deadweight foot
he dragged behind him when he brought your groceries out.
He started walking fine soon after Lily
prayed over him. And by the 4th he was
running the sack race at the annual picnic.
And Widow Black who had the rheumatism
so bad she couldn't sew or knit, took up
the needlecraft again in time to make
some samplers for the county fair. So there
is that. I think it was the sympathy
that helped to heal them all. I think that Lily
just cared enough for God to notice it.

Well, like I said, the healing kept up all week,
maybe six, seven hours every day.
At supper time her Daddy told them all
to leave. He'd stand there with his gun and say,
"I'll shoot whoever tries to hang around

and there won't be no healing after that."
I don't know if he thought that it was real,
the healing, but I doubt he did, then. Just
figured he'd have to deal with it awhile
and then, he guessed, it all would fizzle out.

It tired Lily awfully bad to heal
all day like that, and so her mamma kept
her in the house whenever they was done
with healing for the day. But I snuck over
to see her while my parents read the scripture
and dozed off in the evening time. I snuck
up to the little window at the back
side of the house, where Lily slept, and called
her name real soft. I whispered with her there,
me standing on a bucket turned upside-
down, her leaning her forehead on the screen
until it left little squares in her skin.
The lightning bugs drifted by like glowing snow
or like they was the last embers from a long
burned out grass fire. The wind, for once, was still.
I asked her what she thought about when she
was healing, and she said that she just felt
their hurt and asked for God to give the thing
they obviously needed, like if their leg
was broke then she just said, Oh God, Oh Lord
please fix this leg. And that was it.

I took to heart her words and started praying too.
Mostly I prayed for her big brother, Sam,
who went to fight the big war overseas.
He was a good eight years ahead of us,
but still we girls cooked up this plan for him
and me to marry and us to be sisters.
He was a whole lot softer than his daddy was,
thin, quiet, with a mop of curly blonde
on top. I don't think that he cared for school
that much, or for his daddy's farm. I thought
he'd be a preacher, maybe, but the war
broke out and he ran off to join the fight.
I guess he'd had enough of his farm chores
and harsh words from his daddy. I prayed that
he would come home unhurt, for several nights
after that one, and I told Lily so
she prayed too, even after all day long
praying for all those other people's hurt.
Well, by the end of that same week, Sam came
home, but he didn't come at all unhurt.
I can't say that we wasn't heard by God,
only I guess He had some other plans.

They brung him home with one leg missing
and a big bandage wrapped around his ribs.
They had to fetch him down from the City,
him stretched out in the back of the wagon.
They took Lily along to pick him up,
so all the healing had to stop while they

was gone. Before they left, his daddy waved
his shotgun at the crowd and said, "Get off
my land, and don't be here when I get back."
It took them two whole days to get there, track
him down, and bring him home, so things were quiet
a little while. Most people kept their sick
and injured home. The whole town stood stock still
it seemed to me. With Lily gone, I had
no one to play with and no miracles
to watch, so I clung close to home, listened
to Mamma talk with other ladies all
about the healings and the war and such.

It was real late when they got home. I heard
the wagon rumble by and somehow knew
that it was them. I slipped out with my ma
and pa asleep and crept down to their house
to hide behind a tree and watch them bring
Sam in.

    I saw his daddy lift him up
from in the wagon bed. Sam looked so small.
His eyes was closed, and he looked like a baby
there in his father's arms, though I don't know
his daddy ever held him when he was
a baby. Held him then though, picked him up
out of the wagon and started to walk
into the house but stopped there in the yard
and stood still. He just held him with the moon

spilling white light on them in the front yard
for just a minute, with Sam's ma and Lily
looking at them. And then they all went in
and I was left alone in the dark yard.

I waited for a real long time until the lights
went out, and then I snuck around to whisper
through Lily's window. But she wasn't there.
Instead I saw that they had laid Sam out
there on her bed. His bandage shined like white-
water in the moonlight. It was too hot
for blankets or for too much clothes, so I
could see the wound real clear, also the stump
of leg. I heard him moan like a new calf
and wanted to reach out and stroke his hair.
I didn't even think to pray for him.

When I walked back into the trees, Lily
was waiting there for me. It seems no one,
for once, was paying much attention to her
or where she was. They was all worried
because of Sam. She told me how his wound
had got infected while they shipped him home
and how his fever made him talk. "Angels,
there was pale angels in the trenches," he
would say. I stayed all night there in the yard
with her, and no one said a word when they
found us asleep there in the morning, except
"Come in and get some breakfast." Later I
sure got it good when I got home, though.

Well, people started coming around again
wanting to be healed, but Lily's daddy stood
there on the porch with his shotgun, without
a word sending them all away. If pushed,
he'd say, "You have to pray your own prayers now.
We'll look out for our own, and you can do
the same." I saw then that his meanness weren't
a kind of hate, you know. It was a kind
of love. A fierce and scared love he'd locked up
inside his chest. I guess that Sam might have
turned out the same, if he had lived. Love makes
a gentle man turn rough and sharp sometimes,
if it gets stirred up with too much of worry.

The rest of this I didn't see, but Lily
told it to me a little later on.
Another week or so Sam laid there in
that bed and talked out of his mind. Lily
had took to sleeping on the front porch swing,
and one night toward the end, she said, her daddy
woke her before the sun came up, softly
shaking her shoulder while she slept. His eyes,
she said, looked all wrung out, as if he had
been crying. She had never seen him cry.
He scooped her up and carried her inside,
back to the room where Sam was all laid out.
He didn't say a word, just set her down
beside Sam's bed and looked at her until
she knew he wanted her to pray. She squeezed

her hands together hard enough to leave
marks from her nails that looked like little moons.
She said she kept on kneeling there in prayer
until the sun was up, the whole long time
her daddy standing over her. She thinks
she must have fell asleep sometime. She woke
up in her parents bed a little after lunch,
sweating from the dry heat.

                That afternoon
Sam died. They buried him behind the church,
the last time for six months or more I saw
that family at that place. But then, at last,
her mamma started church-going again
and Lily too, and then, to my surprise,
I saw her daddy sitting in a pew,
one Sunday, with his eyes aimed down, his arms
folded across his chest. I heard him say
to my pa standing after church beneath
the sycamore that shades the bare churchyard,
that if the Lord was real in all that healing,
which anyone would have to say He was,
then He must be as real in all the loss
and suffering too, and maybe that can be
enough, or maybe it will have to be.

She didn't do no more of healing, though.
And mostly no one asked, except for now
and then someone showed up with a sick child

or old, lame person. They was sent away
with bread and jam or maybe with a pie,
some prayer, I guess, but no clear miracle.

The big old stage with all the chicken wire
sat in the yard for quite awhile until
it got torn down a little at a time
to patch up this or that. They always had
a lot of things that needed patching up.

Reading Group Discussion Questions

1. According to Will, "Every farmer knows you carry what you lose." How do the various characters "carry" their loss?
2. Compare and contrast the voices of the various characters. What does their speech reveal about them?
3. Discuss the Reverend and his role in the community. How is he similar/different from other characters?
4. Discuss Louise and what her perspective reveals about the effects of the Dust Bowl.
5. How does Louise's voice and character contrast with those of her mother?
6. Henry's exit from the book is mysterious. What do you think is his fate?
7. Why do you think the poet chose the sonnet form to tell this story?
8. How does "The Faith Healer" change your perspective on the character of Louise?
9. Speculate on why the poet separated the book into two parts. How do these two parts differ?
10. How does Myers' account of the dust bowl differ from Steinbeck's famous version in *The Grapes of Wrath*?